FAITH LOST AND FOUND

Jim Hanson

Cyberwit.net
HIG 45 Kaushambi Kunj, Kalindipuram
Allahabad - 211011 (U.P.) India
http://www.cyberwit.net
Tel: +(91) 9415091004
E-mail: info@cyberwit.net

Printed at Repro India Limited.

Why are you afraid? Have you no faith?

– Jesus, Mark 4:40

If no doubt existed, no faith would be needed.

– John Caputo, Acts of Religion

The world is a spirit vessel

which cannot be acted upon.

– Tao Te Ching, 29

INTRODUCTION

Faith is part of being human: faith in the religious texts of Moses and Jesus in the Bible, Saint Augustine's *Confessions*, Dante's *Divine Comedy,* and Milton's *Paradise Lost/Regained*; in modern texts of Martin Buber's *I and Thou*, Paul Tillich's *Systematic Theology,* Anne Frank's diary, Martin Luther King's speech "I Have a Dream", and Mahatma Gandhi's "Quit India"; and in Eastern texts of *Tao Te Ching,* Buddhist sutras, Rumi's poems, and Hindu *Bhagavad Gita.* We all have some faith in our selves and in the social/cultural realm, bio-physical realm, and ideal gods and heavens – some transcendental faith beyond who we are and what we know.

Yet given the finitude of human life and mind, faith is doubtful, perhaps mindless futility, like Sisyphus pushing his rock with great effort and no outcome, oscillating between resolution and dissolution, redemption and sin, nirvana and samsara. Doubt persists in all inquiries including poetry: Is the end another exalted beginning as promised by T.S. Eliot, or the futility lamented by Sylvia Plath and John Berryman? Perhaps the finding and losing of faith is an unending process.

Contents

1. FAITH LOST

PLACES

Places stay unmoved
empty and silent
unchanged and timeless
lasting and lifeless,
like Easter Island
monoliths out in space,
like pyramid chambers
of pharaohs within

and places have spaces to fill
for people to come and go
in long files with straight lines
each to replace who came before

and people to have a face
with countenance tailored
by a suit and dress code
fashioned to the place filled.

So people flow through years
en route to their careers
to find in the wasteland
glass ceilings and low floors

their faces in train windows
passing by still and staid
on bodies through turnstiles
counted by demographers

their bodies filling in places
for fitting into office desks
and crouching in assembly lines

ever calling to come and stay
nine to five counted on the clock
added as life hours to work

in places of blunt destiny
lived out to be conforming fate
when a born baby cried too late.

TRAIN NEVER CAME

Born in a heartland town
not left for city life

wrote a column in the paper
once named citizen of the year

lived alone in quiet
grew old before his time

with no hope or dream to heed
took to walking night-time streets

dreaming of a lustrous place of
another time and life to live.

Then one day they heard him say,
he had to find another life
a thousand miles anywhere
to be

where he listened for a train
its clamor and calling horn
to come

when to hear sounds of hope
to ride on boundless rails
to go.

Each morning at the station
he sat silent on a bench

looking down tracks more narrow
down tracks on worn wooden ties

looking down the line of light
showing land of promise

forgetting tracks and station
were abandoned years ago

when hope once came aboard
not too late for destiny.

They took him from the station
to put in a secure home

where not seeing old faces
while looking out the window

and so going back for the train
to escape a future of fate

there on a bench, dressed with suit and tie
ticket and suitcase in hand

ready to go down the line
to start life anew again

until he died still waiting
for the train that never came.

PHOTO ALBUM

You have aged in your
old and tattered clothes
now stained shreds of loose ends

once trim and worn well
for those you courted and loved
who joined to celebrate
youthful looks of future hope
shown in the photo album

now a distant reminder lying
in a desk drawer
you open with care to exult
shining faces of adventure
not seen in the bathroom mirror
when abiding another day
in the baleful routine of pills and bills
exercises and appointments

yet still
you relive those remembrances
of youthful loves and future hopes.

So do it yet still
no matter how torn and worn
you feel, how lost your looks
for those yet to be loved

before too late in time to end,
today to become yesterday
and tomorrow soon to follow.

You cannot stop what is ahead,
and nothing matters when you're dead.

NIGHT RUMINATIONS

Sleepless in the night
I step out on the patio to see
the light of stars and galaxies
billions of light years away in a
universe speeding beyond horizons

and I wonder if there is a
past or future of time to know,
center to start or edge to end
or cause of etiology
or purpose of eschatology.

These are questions asked by old men
whose lives no longer travel roads
to tomorrows taken for granted
and whose minds come to question
the honored texts of proclaiming

gods of the Bible, Qur'an or Vedas
souls transcendent and reincarnated
New Age prophecies and AI infinities
and popular modern philosophies

all honored answers for a
life speeding beyond wonder
that their ruminations of night
will see the beginning of day.

I return to bed and fall asleep
to dream of Dorothy's rainbow journey
beyond the woods and past the witches
following the winding yellow road
to the curtain and booming voice

and hold her hand with hope to
hear truth of a world complete
from a wise and white-haired man
named Jacques Derrida who says:
Nothing exists beyond the text.

NIGHT DOG

Restless thoughts haunt me
lying sleepless in the night
with open books on the floor

and hearing the old dog growl
from out of the dark and into my mind
– or is it from my mind into the dark?

Either way, fear lurks here
and I get up to walk out
to leave dark thoughts behind

yet the stalking, no escape
from shadows moving behind –
or is it me imagining light ahead?

Come day, I read and ponder books
with questions of ultimate concern
and for answers still to find and learn:

no cosmological answer that
worlds before and after life
survive in the universe

no thermodynamic answer that
matter in black holes is conserved
to resist against entropy

no theological answer that
souls and heavens exist
beyond this ephemeral world

no anthropic answer that
I exist because of
nature's purpose for me

no apotheotic answer that
I exist because of
god's creation of me

no ontotheological answer that
god exists because of
my idea of god.

Better not to answer now,
not to answer in the night
dangerous questions in the day

questions leaving only doubt
gnawing at my existence,
clawing at walls in my mind.

Better to seek peace unperturbed
like a clam unmoved, unmovable
basking in the givenness of day.

Dogs do not eat clams, or do they?
I walk quietly on through the night
careful to let the sleeping dog lie.

DEMONS

Demons hoary and haunting speak
through residue of lore and tales,
in childhood memories buried
to relieve past shame and secrets

rising unseen as noxious fumes
through floors of present conceits,
attacking ego defense mechanisms
and havens of adult rationality

fluttering as a sweet butterfly
and taking nectar from flowers,
devoured later by a transformed
worm unseen in camouflage green

resounding in eerie forms of fear,
heard in an awakening hour
as wolves howl under the moon and
clutch the night before dawn of day

heard by those huddling around the fire
as children sing their song of trust,
"The wolf sleeps at day to play at night,"
knowing demons come alive if believed.

The light of dawn shines forward
to show the way to refuge
and rid the danger of demons
who fade away at morning light

no longer creatures of fateful doom
as told in stories of being slain
by heroes with a thousand faces
to save humanity in their day.

Yet in our day of ego assurance
the legend of the Minotaur still bides
as human-animal monster conceived

by the Minos queen and white bull
to conceal in the labyrinthine
and hide human shame and deceit

disregarded by adults to be
stories believed only by children
whose demons lie below the mind where

the id coils the amygdala,
sleeping with one eye open
to lunge up and take the soul.

DEMON OF HATE

The fire of hate blows across the
landscape of human desire
and burns truth, beauty and goodness,
fueled by oxygen of damnation
and lit by the spark of emotion
to burst the fabric of civilization:

rising from the unconsciousness of
Freud's lust and shame of rapacious passion,
Oedipus and Electra complexes
burning through the firewall of repression

exploiting interests in the conflict
of Hegel's master-slave relation,
contentment of master with status quo
resentment of slave with no place to go

conquering territories to thrive as
Darwin's fittest to kill and eat,
exterminating brutes to survive
in Joseph Conrad's heart of darkness,
breaking ecological balance
for biological dominance

determining free spirit through
Laplace's demon to put down
hope for a future destiny
into the fate of the past

acquiring knowledge of evil with good
as innocence lost in Bible's Eden,
exiled to a world of original sin
where brother murdered brother and
Jesus crucified on the cross.

The match was struck in Eden
and the fire blew through limbo,
down upon the innocent
damned by sin and passion

suffering spread everywhere
seen by those with open eyes
the dead denied by the blind

hatred scorching verdant land
sixth extinction now at hand

warning written in black sand.

HOMO BEAST

The beast in the amygdala lies coiled
silent, watchful and easily aroused
by movement of nature's ancient rivals

   to strike against threats to genetic purity
   to stride forward for territoriality
   as males kill males for breeding intra-species
   as males unite for killing inter-species

   triumphs after the homo species
   evolves from the hominid genus
   stands erect, club in hand, enlarged brain
   talks zoolingua to coordinate action.

The species numbered nine when
crossing the continents of earth
three hundred thousand years ago:

   Neanderthals in Europe
   Denisovans in Asia
   Homeo Erectus in Indonesia
   Homo Rhodesiensis in central Africa
   Homo Naledi in south Africa
   Homo Luzonesis in Philippines
   Home Floresiensis in Indonesia
   Red Deer Cave in China.

Then nine became one, ten thousand years ago
after Homo Sapiens arrived and killed
the other eight, as told in the remains of

    Ötzi the oldest found preserved in
    Alpine ice, slain and broken by
    hand-crafted arrow and club.

Darwinians expound on the killing
as survival of the fittest, but not as
extermination of all the brutes

    a nineteenth century colonial phrase
    when killing become internecine
    based on god and pigment of skin.

Modern Darwinians expound on food chains in
ecological balance by Keystone Species
safeguarded by Homo Sapiens at the top

    forgetting the other hominids perished
    because we the Homo Sapiens killed them
    down to last mother and baby not like us

    then turned to kill those of and among ourselves
    with odd gods, colored bodies, and alien tongues
    to wage wars of cultures and ideologies
    from the Holocene epoch to the Holocaust.

There is no mystery about evolving life
nor about the extinction of the weaker
by the stronger plants and animals
and by Homo Sapiens stronger still.

The dead brutes remain in the beast brain
so the killer question lingers yet:

Would we still be Homo-neanders
learning about fire, wheel, and seed?

APEX PREDATOR

Nature is a killing and eating campaign
    unstoppable, swirling forward like locusts
        devouring plants below in their path

    sparrows and swallows joining the feast
        upon well-nourished locusts

each making way along the food chain
        predator to prey
        top to bottom

        bottom to top
        balanced feedback

        humans down to worms
        then food for worms.

Then came the epic of Anthropocene
    of the apex predator
    breaking the food chain

        by club in hand
        then spear and gun

    and then the industry of food
    once wild, then tamed to human taste

domesticated on farms
　　the hunted herded
　　the gathered planted

manufactured in factories
　　life under knife
　　slicing plants
　　dicing meats

displayed down grocery aisles
　　leaves of green, meats of red
　　grains processed tan to white
　　under bright neon lights
　　to music of cash registers

Now comes from organized killing fields
civilized eating rites in homes where

　hand with knife and fork
　gives pause for a prayer
　asking bread this day for

　　good weather at farms
　　efficiency in factories
　　low prices of stores

by families thankful to make
incantations first in caves
to seek blessings from God to

　　kill and eat
　　plant and meat.

FORM AND FAITH

Humanity condemned
for building the Tower of Babel,
as the first monument to God
but unrequited for hubris
so the story goes.

Form and faith
once one language by a trusting God
then languages by a punishing God,
so form falls to forms, faith to faiths
contrary, contentious, chaotic.

Civilization devolves
to contending civilizations of
rivers that overflow lands
steel that shatters stone
fire that ignites nuclear
leaders that raise empires
empires that raze civilizations.

Humanity marches to the brink
of the abyss and sixth extinction
and brings the Anthropocene Age
overpopulating the earth
trampling life and despoiling the land
poisoning water and polluting air.

Humanist forms fall into chaos
and fail to provide steadfast meaning:

linguistic form deconstructs as
algorithms digitalize meaning
social media chat trivia,
hieroglyphic icons return
according to the Rebus Principle

artistic form degenerates as
the transcendent yields to entertainment
Rachmaninoff's concertos fading into silence
before the noise of Broadway musicals
and da Vinci's precision drawings
before Pollack's streams of chaos,
all yielding to dissidence
of postmodernist pathos

natural form perishes as
rain forests are burned for fields
fields by suburban sprawl
native populations displaced
wild life exterminated,
civilizations clashing through the ages
by West against East, North against South

biological form disappears as
genetic transformation of DNA
cells parted and organisms modified,
life modified and engendered
by the engineers of science

intellectual form succumbs to
generative retraining transformation
and by codes of zeros and ones,
making brainless machines to
manage civilization.

As forms of nature and culture dissolve
before the urgency of brute conflict
and agency of greed and dominion,

faiths clash on the road of perfidy
once taken by Paul to Damascus and
now by the beast slouching to Bethlehem

the Phoenix remains in ashes
as the fire of faith fails to save
the last of civilizations.

FATAL FLUTTER

So it was to be:
God created
Mindful humanity
Universal law
World without flaw
Amen.

So it came to be:
Butterfly fluttered
Wind rippled
Earth shuttered
World crippled
So be it.

2. RESIDUE

DARK RESIDUE

Residue stays, throughout your days
never to choose, never to loose
there as the dark dwelling in you:

Karma gathers as crust
around the self aging
ever thick and corrosive,
one skin laid on another
but unlike the tidy snake
never shedding them away,
letting nothing to shine
from within or outside,
except when provoked to
unleash protective fangs
of self identity,
and hiding in dark
within old age doubt,
covering the hardened heart
of a self becoming frail
and feeling more mortal.

I begin again walking the
Twelve Steps one at a time
my glass left empty behind
to break addictive habits
and to quench obsessive needs,
but I stumble and fall
a step from the wagon
as binge turned to bender

and regress into hell,
my life lost from the
way once dry and clear
with no one to fear
but my self.

The grime of infamous time
crackles beneath heavy feet
marching into barb-wire camps,
to fenced-in square buildings
with barred windows and steel doors
and chimneys with emissions
dismal and malodorous
to rise and fall to the ground,
leaving only charcoal crust
to crackle beneath heavy feet
marching again – do you hear it?

He finally was voted away
but left with the flick of a match
a wildfire burning across the land
turning once fertile fields of green
barren and black under a cloud,
as institutions smoldered from
forces of heated hate and malcontent
leaving behind for generations ahead
the remains of a republic uncertain
to rise in an unforeseeable future.

I tried to stop and rewind the film
to redo the script of a surreal plot
– Hear me out! –
to reread lines of tragic fiction
with the end of what became real,
and to recant and redo the deed

– I love you! –
to save what was not savable
from the burning bridge of hope
and to undo what had been done
– Don't go! –
to stay yet another moment
just to talk about better times
when we were young and lighthearted
and the future was ours to share
– Come back! –
and the question won't stop:
What happened that night?

The dead never die
as their spirit lives
to inhabit the world,
moving from past to present
sideways out of vision
in light out of facades
from faraway mirrors,
shimmering in an old movie
pale characters looking out
and speaking silent truth
in the once forgotten past
of renewed nostalgia,
standing in public statues
and speaking through revered books
to project their legacies
for generations to believe
in the life of their legends,
riding aurora borealis
as souls to escape from sins
on earth to be forgotten
and free to flee away.

BRIGHT RESIDUE

Residue stays, throughout your days
never to choose, never to loose
there as the light dwelling in you:

I remember her well
her beautiful body
and picture-perfect mind,
like Leonard Cohen's Suzanne
etched at the time
in my imperfect mind
wanting to travel with her
and wanting to travel blind,
so we did together
swept away by the wind
into spaces and times
of forms joined and perfect,
now seen in old photos
and letters read with love
still kept in my room to
remember her once here.

The Parthenon still survives
through the passing of ages
once one of seven wonders
in an early storied world,
dedicated to Athena and
goddesses of its caryatids
bespeaking feminine glory,
celebrated as a beacon of

virtue, beauty and civility
where free citizens debated
human rights of a republic,
scattered now as broken stone
abandoned on a high hill
as the remains of today to
show civilization the way.

When my boyhood dreams of taking
the highway of adventures were
lived as events in a funeral home
among people as rocks of all ages
with faces in newspaper obituaries,
I traveled east up the state highway
to cities of opportunity
– college degree, resume, jobs,
careers, annuities, rented rooms,
passing voices slurred, faces blurred –
and when talking to nameless people
I began to whisper to myself
– leave this noisy place
and everyone belonging
to somewhere else, and
go back where you belong –
so I came home to stay where
the streets went to known places
and to people having last names
and faces in high school yearbooks.

White cotton in blue sky
flutters down through the air
breathed out by green trees
breathed in by brown ground

ingested and sprouted out
then returning to air,
in and out to rise and fall
always there in timeless flux
throughout the cycle of change,
as residue still not gone
repeating what was of life
in the past wanting to last.

Whitman's song of self partakes you
to filter and fibre your blood
through your heart and into your soul
through day and into the night
shining out to the world beyond,
and you know now still in this time
across the land of boundless space
he sits along the open road
in body turned to leaves of grass
always somewhere waiting for you.

The lotus floats
untethered
from the earth of samsara,
high upon the water
without effort
already there,
always when
sat upon by Brahma
before the beginning,
its spirit ever blooming
still beyond the end.

The wind is the voice of God
as the Ultimate Residue
constant, unchanging
cosmic, origin unknown
instantaneous, absolute
ubiquitous, inexhaustible
formless, empty,
yet it brings calmness
to your restless soul,
so listen and you will hear it
come from beyond the universe
into the channels of your mind.
Do you hear it?
    Try easier.

3. ANTHROPIC FAITH

ANTHROPIC PRINCIPLE

Life in the universe is
possible in trillions but
    only one known
    just ours by us

and other lives unknown
too far and small to see
    like ants in holes
    just theirs by them

life just theirs by them known
through time-space at light speed
on some exo-planet shown
beings odd and strange to see

    deflated by gravity
    and inflamed by heat
    life inscrutable
    forms immeasurable

    arbitrary as God rolling dice
    likely as a lone neutrino
    futile as Chinese boxes

    in a strange universe
    unknown and unalike

    with endless possibility.

Life unknown to be known is possible
from the Anthropic Principle, whether:

Weak principle, uncertain universe
human life an accident to survive:

> a freak left behind others
> like a dead-end dinosaur
> just before a meteorite
>
> or a jar on a Tennessee hill
> with weeds of nature rising around
> yet there out of place and lost in time
>
> unfit to thrive according
> to laws of evolution
> but still trying to survive
>
> anomalous and vulnerable
> temporary locality.

Strong principle, certain universe
human life of the many as model:

> oneness known by ancient mystics
> trusting in a world humanized
> praying to heaven with Jesus and
> meditating in nirvana with Buddha
>
> completeness of Periodic Table
> featuring life elements normalized
> to exist on exoplanets moving
> along countless Cinderella paths

infinity of the human mind
extended by a neural network
like Indra's Net of fractal jewels
sparkling across the universe

mutual immanence
as said by Whitehead
the world in us
and we in the world.

So asks the anthropic question:

Are we one of few in a trillion
or in a trillion of all as one?

ANTHROPIC LEGENDS

The world was ours as first told
in Axial Age legends of old,
the planets as spiritual spheres and
the stars as vigilant and caring gods
ruling over wanton worlds below,
so told for ages after as always
seen through anthropic eyes:

by ancient Greeks as *psyche tou kosmo*
Latins as *anima munde*
Hindus as *parama puru[a*

by Dante and the Bible
sometimes damned as hell
sometimes blessed as heaven

by modern English as life force
French as *elan vital*
German as *lebengeist*

when Adam and Eve joined
in the gardens of antiquity
to taste the apple tree of knowledge
or enticed by pagan spirit
to hear Erato play the harp

when young Lakota warriors met
the White Buffalo woman who
taught seven prayer ceremonies

and left behind a sacred bundle
radiating wisdom and peace

when the giant Pangu of Tao
with head at sky and feet on earth
took ax in hand to break the egg shell
holding chaos and set free to put
out the yen and yang in harmony

when Shiva left the lotus flower
and came upon the *maya* world
to confront human-created
edges of space and lapses of time
and to dance to its destruction, and

knowing all the while with a smile
we float through an ether of
dark energy and matter
unknown even by our science,
still trusting in anthropic legends
of the big bang by a cosmic egg.

ANTHROPIC QUALMS

Is nature your anthropic friend
or spiritual inspiration?

Look up above and think again
starting with the universe.

The world is not the idea
said to be only in the head
of you and Schopenhauer
who live but a brief moment
as a small ant climbing Mount Everest
and if venturing five miles high
to die instantly,

and you and Carl Sagan
are not gloried star stuff
because you will never see
any star having even one
drop of blood
fiber of flesh
or piece of bone,

and you and Edwin Hubble will
never contact life on
exoplanets billions
of light years away,
not for you to see them
or them to see you,

and you and Elon Musk
really wanting to inhabit Mars
without sufficient oxygen,
with water only on the south pole
and where median temperature is
100 degrees below Fahrenheit

and not even gods want to be among
planets and asteroids colliding,
stars exploding in silent violence,
supernovae emitting gamma rays,
or galaxies speeding into infinity

all of this recognized in
ancient Chinese straw dogs
made up and blessed
then put to fire and thrown in streets,
to placate nature's indifference
to its ten thousand sentient beings.

ANTHROPIC TAOISM

Heaven and Earth are not humane.
They treat ten thousand beings as straw dogs.
– Tao Te Ching, 5

The ancient Chinese understood nature
to host the living as a killing field,
so appeased its gods by dismembering dogs
and putting their parts before town gates
to quell the hunger of dragons
lurking outside to feed on flesh
and wanting to return inside
to fears of starvation and death

so after Confucian piety
ancients sacrificed dogs made of straw,
burned and thrown away in the street
where dragons accepted on the inside
ran still hungry and became angry,
breaking down the civil confines of
states and waging war for two centuries

yet Taoist nature never cared
(the dragons not its creation)
for dogs of red flesh or burned straw,
never the friend of dog or man,
never to respond to the call
of humane living and dying

and Taoists never knew nature
by names ever lasting or
by names known by opposites,
rather knew through the yin and yang
of life known to be life as death and
order known to be order as chaos.

Taoists know what not to know
about delusions of human mind,
about harmony of life and death
and what buoyant buddhas say
on suffering to go away and
we today know as Halloween

that nature is about itself
not about humans and their mind
as now known by science as:
creation and destruction
light speed and energy
entropy and atrophy, also
death of dragons, dogs and humans.

ANTHROPIC PLEA

Ever seeking

you far away,

out some where in

the universe,

of empty space

and countless time,

wanting the same

for what is real,

to know you exist

in some form,

whether a god

as primal force,

of all that came

and comes to be,

and a person

much like me,

a face or voice

to see or hear,

a conscious mind

of word and thought,

love and justice

found everywhere,

no matter where

to join with you,

as lost children

found together,

by contact made

and not alone.

THE HONKING OF THE GEESE

With the seasons life passing by
comes the haunting honking of the geese
honk, honk, honking to say all is well

echoing across mountains and valleys
riding the jet stream over oceans
in v-formations cutting through clouds
up against wind, storms, and searing cold

strong wings on frail bodies
stalwart ever endless
straight forward without dread
two thousand miles ahead.

From ground-bound human dominion
their winged migration can be charted
as specks moving across radar screens
tracked as missiles to start human war

yet they steer on time-known trails
unerring without GPS
knowing where to go without thought

freely free over rows of tamed farmlands
hungry for food found in drained wetlands
close among skyscrapers of cities
through rising smoke funnels of factories
into soiled clouds and waters below

still seen in graying sky
to return to the nest
where we all go to rest.

4. AXIAL AGE

AXIAL DAWN

Arise now, arise, thou great noontide.
Friedrich Nietzsche, Thus Spake Zarathustra

The dawn was seen that axial day
　　not just light alone
　　on forgotten earth
　　for life waking blind

　　but something more
　　beyond the light of day
　　into the night still seen

The third eye of mind came to see
　　　not just things passing
　　　seen on cave wall facades
　　　then silver screen websites

　　　but of things surpassing
　　　travails of rushing time
　　　details of pressing space

　　　Zarathustra descending
　　　from newfound heights of vision
　　　to proclaim a perfect world.

The great wakening of
　　consciousness
　　transformative

    infinite
    beyond
    god.

The great making of
    civilization
    transcendence
    language
    morality
    humanity.

FIRST AXIAL AGE

May we live in interesting times
that clever Chinese curse and yet
a disingenuous boast of the
American Century and belief in
exceptionalism and end of history.

Every time is most interesting
to the people who live in it
and pledge steadfast allegiance to
laud the importance of their age
and the virtue of their empires

to save humanity of the Twentieth
enraged by two hot world wars
with tens of millions dead and
and one war cold with lucky rolls
of thermonuclear dice

to savage nature of the Twenty-first
waged by humans eight billion and more
spewing over the land and other life
to despoil earth, water, air and fire
to feed the fat in a new flat world.

So goes the Anthropocene Age of
modern pride and industrial pillage,
yet more nobler centuries may be found:

my heart in the Nineteenth
of Beethoven, Nietzsche, Marx, Darwin .
to feel the power to change by treason

my head in the Eighteenth
of Bach, Goethe, Hume, Voltaire
to feel the power to arrange by reason.

My spirit goes back in the Axial Age
twenty-five tumultuous centuries ago
when Yeats' ceremony of innocence began
with Socrates, Zoroaster, Buddha and Lao Tzu
as the best having all conviction to watch
over the worst filled with passionate intensity:

back to the mysterious coincidence
(perhaps the work of unknown providence)
when Greeks debated thoughts along the Aegean Sea
Arabs recited gathas on the Persian desert
Indians meditated under the Bodhi tree
Chinese ate the analects of Tao in rice bowls

those who came, saw and transcended with care
the totems and taboos of pagan charm
who sought the higher and found salvation
who spoke truth and forged civilization.

Oh Jaspers
take me back to that Axial Age
when the world was of the sage
and the future came from the past
and the truth found would always last.

SECOND AXIAL AGE

Western or Eastern civilization
both owe sages of forgotten ages

   as recurring beacons
   arising with the sun

   to brighten dark periods
   and light civilization.

Best known the First Axial Age of
   twenty-five centuries ago.

Less known the Second Axial Age of
   eight centuries ago:

   Aquinas and universities of Natural Theology
with Anselm as father of Scholasticism
following Socrates and Aristotle

   Zen trinity of Dogen's zazen
with Huikai writing the Mumonkan
and Nichiren holding Pure Land lotus
following the Buddha

   Golden Age of Tao
with ruling Tang and Song dynasties
extolling the Tao and Analects
following Lao Tzu and Confucius

Rumi and the Divine Love of Sufism
with Arabic conceiving the Unity of Being
following Zoroaster.

We again live dangerously
  in an interesting time

    of shameless greed
    democracy sold

    of timeless terror
    justice annulled

    continents soiled
    in blood

    environment razed
    by fire.

Civilization struggles to survive
before another age of darkness

to restore purity of faith
and surety of communion

to abide again in the light
provided by another sage

to follow the first and second
with the Third Axial Age.

THEN AND NOW: LESSONS FROM THE AXIAL AGE

History does not repeat, but it does instruct.
– Timothy Snyder, On Tyranny

The more determinedly I exist, as myself, within the condi-
tions of the time, the more
clearly I shall hear the language of the past, the nearer I
shall feel the glow of its life.
 – Karl Jaspers, On My Philosophy

They came down the axial road
at the dawn of civilization

in the light of their consciousness
for a new world of human making

Lao Tzu with Confucius from the East
Socrates with Plato from the West

ere the twain met united to speak
under the Bodhi Tree of Jetta Grove

where the Buddha sat smiling and calm
greeting his guests on that golden day of
the fifth century BCE of the Axial Age

when the world was of the sage
and the future came from the past
and the truth found would always last.

Buddha: Welcome good friends
and thank you for your travel from
societies now rising as cities and
civilizations inspiring people
enlightened by new-age consciousness,
though I must add that few are contented
due to suffering from the three poisons
of greed, hatred and delusion
and from ignorance about the
four noble truths and eight-fold path.

Socrates: Yes, they rise and speak
in emerging city-states of
worship, commerce and government,
yet still stay in caves to see
mere reflections of the real
on the wall as a medium
of flashing images from forums
used by servers of self-deceit,
as Atlas shrugging off truth and
letting the world fall asunder.

Plato: They revel at the rhetoric
of sophists who inveigh against
Socrates and the democratic republic,
who claim to speak for common citizens
yet come from families of wealth
and academies of privilege
to seek tyranny by promising
to make Athens great again.

Lao Tzu: The people think only
of righteous laws and divisive issues

extolled by the Yellow Emperor
who ruled not by love but by law
and praised thought about what is not,
who lied and promoted desire
and created fake faces and books
and spoke with artificial intelligence.

Confucius: They fall prey to *ch'i*
mismanaged by ill-advised rulers
and exploited by tyrants who wage war
as Spring now descends to Autumn
of what may be our warring states,
governing not by goodness and virtue
but by saying their war will end war
when loyalty to state triumphs
over fealty to family and ancestry.

Buddha: True, we live in a time
made perilous by empires such as
founded by Cyrus and the pharaohs,
who no longer find peace in the
theistic teachings of Zoroaster
and Moses now no longer with us
and who threaten war on those
who found refuge in Canaan.

Plato: And states aspiring
to be empires and world guardians
abuse their citizens with high taxes
and shortages of goods and high prices,
provoking libertarian discontent
and arousing populist support
for liars and insurrectionists,

causing democracy and timocracy
to yield to tyranny and oligarchy
thereby persecuting those who
seek open and free dialogue.

Confucius: Warring states will
reject advice of sages and
heed only the voice of Guan Yu,
rejecting peace for waging war
building a great protective wall,
and enlisting in high office
acolytes and opportunists
who profit from emoluments
from rich princes and rogue states.

Socrates: The states govern
in temples and palaces alike
to worship Zeus and minor gods,
using the power of government
to exploit religious zeal and
urging playwrights and sophists
to rue dialogues of reason
used by philosophers to rule.

Lao Tzu: The states contrive
images of gods living in
forgiving and timeless heavens,
denying their humanized existence
is preceded by the primal *tao*
and formless *khôra* of Plato.

Buddha: To be sure, the world
is constructed in consciousness

of the sentient mind that itself
is the nirvana of heaven on earth
and maitreya of consciousness
to bring world peace and compassion.

Plato: The philosopher king may bring
temperance to sophist-incited citizens,
quell their distemper of democracy
and uphold the republic by teaching
civics and citizenship and virtues of
wisdom, courage, moderation and justice.

Lao Tzu: Yet the true sage suspects
elite scholars and legalists extolling
imperatives of rights and duties,
partisan campaigns of dissent,
so opts to rule by inaction
of primitive simplicity
and by silence and example
in place of contention and law.

Buddha: The bodhisattva also avoids
conflicting action and contention,
and by meditation and practice
seeks to free people from desire
and attachment to public dogma,
leading them in silence to the
pure land that gives birth to
the free-floating lotus flower.

Confucius: As the lotus shines with
spiritual awakening and freedom,
jên blossoms as a flower with

spiritual virtue in those who
hear the wisdom of the sage and
rule without resort to force or fraud
and without inciting conflict,
as the grass bends in wind and
water flows down on lowlands.

Socrates: Virtue is of the soul
to be clarified in dialogue
and upheld in law by the city-state
in pursuit of eternal ideas
and the indivisible republic
to bring liberty and justice for all.

Lao Tzu: Yet there remains
the inhumane force of *te*
more natural and felt
than human and taught,
for as humans come from earth
earth comes from heaven
heaven comes from *tao,*
so all comes from the *te* of *tao,*
as the unnamed and unknown cause
of beings and doings on earth.

Plato: Thus we come to
this place to find truth and virtue
as humankind comes to this earth,
evolved with language for thought
and blessed by the eternal flame
of Hestia the virgin goddess
of hearth, home and family.

Buddha: Though the dawn of
civilization seen and revered
may devolve into the night
dimmed by future ignorance,
the axial spirit may rise again
by the second coming
of the maitreya in the East
and the messiah in the West
to meet in the twain of all times.

They came to the bodhi tree
on dawn of that axial day
to contemplate enlightenment
of civilization then and now

arising from the human darkness
in a feral and nescient earth
to speak of truth and compassion

not of power over nature
subjected to their dominion

but about human communion.

5. THEISTIC FAITH

TILLICH'S GOD OF BEING

God does not exist, so said by
Tillich acolyte of Heidegger
and messianic believer who
journeys into Being to find God

making his way past the forms of
existence contrived by humans
and into the infinity
of no form and no existence

as the intrepid voyager
passing the form of Christian God
of self, ego and avatar
to find a remote ontic God

shunning the Father God of Jesus
the avatar confined to known form
for the God of nonexistence
as the infinite of non-form

but believing in the God of Genesis
lighting void and darkness of no form
creating heaven and earth of form
then begetting living beings

and believing in an active God
that addresses ultimate concerns
through Kairos in a moment
of faith known to be eternal

when the event of passing time
becomes the eternal moment
of all seeking and searching
for the absolutes of truth.

God is being itself, he said
for beings themselves to have
knowledge of cosmology
from the faith of ontology.

SPINOZA'S GOD OF NATURE

Spinoza's God abides
in plain sight right here
as close as your nose

not out in Heaven
here in Nature

plants blooming in his light and
animals breathing in his air

maybe an ant breeding
or human redeeming.

His God is Nature unbounded
unlimited in myriad things
the stuff of stars composing us

all particles of energy
and elements of matter

all measured space and time
and forms of mass and mind.

His God of Mind is substance
extended through endless modes
with infinite attributes

this stream of words and numbers
discovering the laws of

elements of the Periodic Table
and particles of the Standard Model

laws and constants governing the
universe of Nature and Mind.

His God of Nature was
deemed dangerous to the
philosophies of then:

Descartes meditating on mind or body
thereby severing them apart

Hobbes prognosticating nature
as a war of all against all

Marx turning Hegel on his head to
endless revolts of class struggle.

So know his God still rankles
in an all-too-human age of
paternal gods and sacred laws

and stands plainly to be seen
in harmony with Nature
and discernment of the Mind.

MOHAMMAD'S GOD OF POWER

You walk with Mohammad
up the trail of barren rock under your feet
and heat of the desert sapping your strength
ascending the mountain of Jabal al-Nour
and entering the remote cave of Hira

and in there take care
when hearing Gabriel speak through walls
the holy word of Allah to prophets
Abraham, Moses, Jesus and
Muhammad anointed last to speak
the Tawhid of "Allah is one."

You look over to see
this last prophet shuddering at hearing the word
scared of his sanity and what the future brings
and there he would pray for three years to renounce
doubt and disbelief until descending the mountain
to preach the word of what would become the Quran

and across the sand
Mohammad is heard and his proclamation
has consequences of conquest and empire
defended and extended against infidels
from ancient Medina to modern Tehran
soaking the desert sand with blood and oil
by a hard forge shaping a harsh religion.

You know this comes
from Plato's caves of mistaken images
or ancient men's caves of arcane worship,
and now heard as the word of Allah to
reverberate in public prayer at dawn
and iterate in five prostrations a day
by two billion people – *Allahu Akbar*.

GOD-HEN

So they say:
the beginning began
with a laid cosmic egg
fourteen billion or so
space-time years ago

by a God-Hen
from another egg
of another God-Hen:
hen of egg or egg of hen,
they know not why or when

except what went wrong
when the Rooster-God
crowed at the dawn:
Let there be light!

Thereby the egg yoke broke
with splatter of matter
from the heat of the light,
an over-fried fright

as omelet galaxies
spun out of grace
faster round and round
then out of space
not to be found

so the Rooster-God
was to be sought
but never caught
to right the wrong.

Because you're here
you know the song:
sitting back on her nest
God-Hen without rest
laid another egg

this time no clatter
no messy splatter
because dark matter
found the right way for
our universe
to stay together
under her feather

without God-Rooster
as crowing booster,
with Father Lemaître
still as true teller

of the story restored
about best laid eggs
for mice and men to
be saved by a hen.

CHASING GOD

God is the tail I chase in a circle
much like a dog mistaking its tail
to no avail as if something else.

For God a circle does not matter
nor my mistaking something else
while attempting to catch myself.

As for me the circle will break
then ending with no beginning
and sending me straight away.

To curve straight lines and corners
I know of no equation
to circle the square, yet

God knows it without fail
while I am the dog
still chasing my tail.

UNKNOWN GOD

What of a personal theistic god who
hears our prayers and responds to your needs,
yet dying from Covid or killed in Ukraine
or mass wipe-out by the rogue planet
in Lars von Trier's movie of Melancholia?

We're past believing that – infamy happens.
The universe is impersonal – to all of us.

What of a knowable deistic God
who acts through laws of science
known not through ontological argument
(from Thomas Aquinas to Paul Tillich)
but through human experience?

We're short believing that – infinity happens.
The universe is unknowable – for all of us.

Science always comes up short,
like Zeno's arrow never reaching its target
and by Kurt Gödel's law of incompleteness
known only through the mystic mathematics of ∞ .

The Big Bang becomes the
last creationist hold-out,
fizzling away without knowledge
of causality or primordiality

and matter and energy
remain dark but for the
abstract light of mathematics
on inexplicable effects

and time-space
extend into infinity
as in Brian Greene's paradox:
until the end of time,
leaving only infinite cycles
without cause or effect.

What of a complete God known in
an incomplete world of unknown?

NO GOD?

No personal God
listens to our prayers or
responds to our pleas.

No moral God allows
collisions and explosions from space
or here on earth epic extinctions
like the coming Yellowstone eruption.

No existential God
is found in space or time
of casuistic beginning
or apocalyptic ending.

Was Leibniz right to ask:
Why is there not nothing?

Given God's absence
he would better ask:
Why is there not God?

Given hypotheticals
he would best ask:
Why is there not why?

Are we right to answer:
There is no why?

6. WESTERN FAITH

HEGEL'S ABSOLUTE

Travelers in time were we
on our way to find truth
with logic and certainty
from Western philosophy

then met a man called Hegel
who expounded upon
thesis and antithesis
to become synthesis,
then synthesis becoming
another thesis and antithesis
to become another synthesis,
up the chain of ideas to
certain truth of the Absolute.

Truth on a chain to
to the Absolute,
was babble we thought
and became skeptics

then we met
Kant and Shlegel
as Platonists
and became idealists

then we met
Feurbach and Marx
as materialists
and became realists

then we met
Sartre and Heidegger
as existentialists
and became sages

way up to truth complete
and the Absolute achieved!

True for ideas, we demurred
(as Westerners concurred)
but what about people
and societies to achieve,

and here too Hegel spoke of
Master and Slave dialectic
to the Absolute idea
of perfect civilization

to arise from the synthesis
of Adam and Eve to family
to clan to kingdom and nation
to society and civilization
modernity and democracy

to end history and ideology
and achieve universality
of Western industrial democracy
as a Kantian hangover
from drinking Enlightenment?

Traveling through more time
seeking factual truth
we found ideas of conflict

and people of greed
and wondered if philosophy
was only ideology

then met a man called Nietzsche
who expounded upon the
antithesis of the Absolute
and the eternal return
past the staid philosophy
of the Last Man to stand.

SANTAYANA'S REALMS

Art is higher than reality and has no direct relation to reality ....
Reality is opposed to the spiritual. – Piet Mondrian
in Michel Seuphor, Piet Mondrian: Life and Work

Santayana the atheist died
after ten years in his bedroom
at a Rome convent where
nuns wept and prayed for his soul,
as he requested awed by their prayer
and entranced with the beauty of ritual.

He expounded in his books on
heavenly essence as best
earthly existence as worst:

essence bright and clean
as the conceived beauty of a flower
remaining as an idea after the flower dies

essential ideas of mind ever-lasting
beyond the existential things of earth,
always as the same by endless name:

Plato's eternal ideas
Spinoza's substance
Hegel's absolute
existence dark and dirty

universes and atoms disentangling
bodies birthing, suffering and dying

existential things of body never-lasting
degrading the essential things of heaven
existence never the same by limited name:

  Derrida's arbitrary text
  Russell's uncertainty
  Einstein's relativity.

He believes in the
supremacy of essence
and beauty of eternal form:

  green always green
  two plus two always four
  qualities and quantities as
  essence of perpetual purity

in essence detached from existence
like a hyacinth floating on water
rootless and free from the ground below

in truth of heaven over earth,
ideals of mind over the facts of matter,
beauty of essence above ugly existence

in Animal Faith to see the world,
only through blind trust of analogic
and instinctive insight of aesthetics.

He cannot answer the question:

Do the forms of divine essence link
to the things of natural existence?

Nature does not speak.
God does not answer.

HEIDEGGER'S OPENING

Martin Heidegger Black Forest philosopher
dwelled in the forbidding forest of the Ardennes

being-there (da-sein) throughout his life
yet moving the world of philosophy

looking for a path through trees and brush
of overgrown rhetoric and metaphysics

to an opening of enlightenment where
beings may see the budding of Being

rising endlessly and moving tirelessly
reflecting the light when passed by attention

from the foundation always there to stay
as self falls away into Nothingness:

    no I of Descartes
    no person of Shakespeare
    no self of Freud or Whitman
    no soul of Plato or Augustine

against language-made perspectives
to deconstruct and cut away:

    not imagined through stories
    not constructed through formulas
    not idealized as eternal ideas
    not weaponized by ideologies

and about philosophies over-thought
to rediscover authenticity:

> not idealized by Hegel's dialectic
> not materialized by Marx's dialectic
> not objectified by Husserl's consciousness
> not limited by Sartre's existence.

He then "turns" back to language to find Being
in the poetry of by Hölderlin about home

to other forms of language shining forth
and beholding natural affirmation

Dasein remains where the light shines
everywhere on things and beings

keeping Being sure and pure by
the Nothingness of openness.

CAMUS'S QUESTION

Albert Camus existential realist
ponders questions of philosophy
and puts all aside, but for suicide:

whether to be or not to be
in a world of no clear meaning
where living has limits on
truth, beauty and goodness

first the futility from death
that does not speak or care,
no living guarantee given

second the absurdity of work
that has no determined outcome,
inflicted upon Sisyphus
pushing his boulder vainly.

So laments Camus
who looses his existential nerve
by wanting nature to be humane
as a purposeful anthropic force
in the service of Ecce Homo.

Like Sartre, he seeks respite from the
freedom of nothingness in nature
which must require responsibility
of being somebody – nobody not an option

for the self must have identity
and the ego its imperative
of dominion over living things,
otherwise nothingness prevails
and life is an absurdity.

So laments Camus, unwittingly
sounding like a Taoist who
throws straw dogs on the street
then tramples and burns them

to heed living absurdly
like the straw dogs treated by
heaven and earth never humane
as a symbolic suicide, to which

the Buddha says, Sit down
Lao Tzu says, Shut up.
Such is life, accept it.

GREAT MAN HISTORY

Historians find faith in heroes
to make stories of history
as novelists find protagonists
whose deeds decide the story

as Homer's heroes of the Iliad
were courageous in destroying Troy
and virtuous in saving Helen,
a fable over fact of how war looks
that launched in history ten thousand books

as heroes march across continents
some as saving princes of peace
most as slaving wagers of war,
stated as creators of events
and unmoved movers like great gods.

History still is displayed today
by professorial dog-owners
trotting out the lineage of presidents
large and small, hairy and lean
each judged by its showing

as great men quoted and toted by
John Meacham and Doris Goodwin
who happily forget flaws and failures
racism and sexism of founding fathers
and corruption of following fathers

as those who keep the faith and ignore the
mega/macro forces that make and break
the foundations of republics and empires,
forces known beyond presidential profiles –

evolutionary struggle of the fittest by Darwin
material struggle of classes by Marx
war of all against all by Hobbs
life cycles of civilizations by Toynbee
dialectics of antitheses by Hegel
cognitive revolution by Harari
sixth likely extinction in Phanerozoic Eon
biblical prophecies of Four Horsemen
or Second Coming of Apocalypse –

no thought given to forces untoward
to the march of events deemed forward,
and their great man will always save
nations of people from themselves.

Thus history is written by makers of WEIRD
(western industrial educated rich democratic)
to behold vaunted values of humanism
(scientific capitalist republican democratic)

and in the troubled world of today
the USA will lead the way to go
and drive the world destined to follow
at the end of the day, as historians say.

GREAT WORLD SCIENCE

World to reset
science journeys into endless frontiers
following Vannevar Bush's call
to chalk equations on squeaky blackboards
and form equations rounding out the world

> from the infinite of astrophysics to
> infinitesimal of quantum physics
>
> from Plato's ideas of certainty to
> Heisenberg's principle of uncertainty
>
> from Newton's and Leibniz's calculus
> to Diderot's encyclopedia
>
> from Darwin's competition of the fittest
> to E.O. Wilson's cooperation of the ants
>
> from Skinner's conditioned behavior
> to Maslow's self actualization.

With no regret
science travels land sea air Internet
to correct thoughts of common experience
debunk myths of traditional insight
and deny beliefs not counted and mounted.

Yet to forget
Lao Tzu's ancient call to loose knowledge
of measured judgments thought to be certain
and attain the quiet harmony of Tao
that gives and takes all things in heaven and earth.

7. EASTERN FAITH

TAO?

There was something nebulous existing
Born before heaven and earth
Silent, empty.
– Tao Te Ching, 25

Plato spoke then of the ideal
and Heraclitus of the real
and philosophers now address
reality and nothingness.

But who in the West
can speak then or now
about the East and
mystery of Tao?

TAO TAUGHT

Tao is a teeter totter
upon which yen and yang play
back and forth and up and down

moving yet present
bestowing balance
holding harmony

known by ancient sages
of the East
sought by modern thinkers
of the West.

Taught by James and Dewey
as the problematic situation
solved by
resistance of yin
resilience of yang.

Taught by Freud
as dark unconscious
of yin
and bright conscious
of yang.

Taught by Sartre
as constitutive consciousness
without ego,
as the nothingness

of yin
and the being
of yang.

Taught by Hegel
as the absolute
of negation
by yin
and affirmation
by yang.

While not of thought
tao still is sought
by words amiss
in ignorance.

TAO!

Mother of earth, origin of yin
gives birth, takes life

before ten thousand beings
seeking birth, avoiding life

before light known and
time-space of universe

beyond perception of senses and
extension of telescopes and microscopes

beyond the conception of mind and
extension of quantum computers

beneath all things of heaven and
depths of measured earth.

Father of heaven, energy of yang
gives heat, shines light

making dark side bright
and land and sky clear

shaping form from infirm bodies
to hold stones and flowing fluids

making immanence manifest
for clarity and calm

making change with the cosmic wind
blowing across the universe

creating life through
uniting of yen and yang.

This Tao as provenance of *te* power:
fifth undetected force in physics
and supersoul of cosmic consciousness,
primal mover of the universe
and preceding images of gods.

This Tao as omnipotence of *ching* change:
I Ching dragon breathing feral fire
Shiva dancing to creation and destruction
Heraclitus citing universal flux
John revealing the apocalypse and return.

Understood by ancient mariners
that their ships would sail off the edge of
the earth into unknown oblivion.

Misunderstood by modern cosmologists
that their scopes would see beyond the edge
of the universe into emptiness.

All missing the timeless mystery of
the unfathomable *te* and *ching* of
the Tao unnamed and everlasting.

YIN AND YANG MEET

In the dark of yin

the earth is stirring

and life arising

in celebration

of yang to unite,

in the light of yang

the flower child blooms

rising to the sun

to give energy

for the birth of yin,

when yin and yang meet

and tao comes complete.

NIRVANA FOUND

At the end of your journey
through the weary karma world

the boundary to cross over
has a gate to enter through

if you find the right path
to leave your self behind,

and once the gate opens
the boundary disappears

and there becomes here
and then becomes now

here and there, now and then
at the start and the end.

Neither gate nor boundary
were ever there to cross.

You live in nirvana,
nirvana lives in you.

NOTHING LOST

You hold onto life but go to nothing.
What do you gain?

You put off death but come from nothing.
What do you lose?

With teeth clinched to a tree branch from a cliff
you are asked what to do to save your life
and you must recite the Lord's Prayer.
How do you say it?

Climbing a one hundred-foot pole
you finally arrive at the top.
How do you advance?

You make a cart with twenty spokes
and take away its box and axle.
What do you have?

You ask what is Buddha
and told shit on a stick.
What do you learn?

You are told the dharma is
no mind, Buddha, or beings.
What do you believe?

You are asked to show your face
before birth and after death.
What do you see?

You seek the koan truth
of nothing feigned or gained:
Nothing lost
      Nothing
          Not
             No
                n
                  ∞

BHRAMARI PRANAYAMA

As the bee sounds making rounds
to Brahma's Kamal flower
I hear humming of my breath,
out and in from death to birth

as the old guru breathes in
the karma of the world and
out the purity of virtue,
transforming suffering to mirth

as does the rhythmic breathing
of life heard in the next room
from my beloved sleeping,
all is still well on this earth.

SHIVA'S DANCE

You want to dance with Shiva
whose aureole circles around you,
standing on the dwarf of ignorance and evil
holding with one hand the fire of change
and with the other the drum of rhythm and time

and entwined by the cobra, fearlessly
to celebrate the cosmos:

to transform its entropic matter
into flames of light and heat from the
fusion and fission of adorning suns
and magnificent, swirling galaxies

to perpetuate its creation and destruction
through the Cyclic Uproar of the Jâtakas,
every one hundred thousand years and
across the three realms of Brahma heaven

to humanize it with purposeful energy
with magic, preservation and emancipation
over eons of creation and destruction

to rule the cosmos
through Brahman consciousness:
eternal and constant beyond
edges of the known universe
where nothing can be known but through
the omniscience of the third eye

and to keep dancing unless
the fire of the aureole burns down
and energy becomes the entropy
of the cosmos gone dark and lifeless.

If too fantastical for you,
then dance with American native ghosts
for the millenarian coming of the past
or dance to the redemptive fires
of the California Redwoods
or dance with Fred Astaire and Ginger to
happy tunes in the thirties depression
or to Leonard Cohen's plea
dance me to the end of love.

What matters is the endless dance,
pulsing through the human heart
to rhythmic cycles of death and life
of lifetimes moving through the ages

and celebration with Shiva,
holder and molder of all worlds
the creator of destruction
and destroyer of creation.

GANDHI'S BELIEFS

A small, skinny man
who was Gandhi
near-sighted
high, squeaky voice
and twig legs
with walking stick

hunched over
frail, fragile
and fasting

prone to collapse
like an old bridge
falling apart,
not to carry his people
across to the other side.

A small, skinny man
who believed and weaved
on an old spinning wheel
the truth of *satya,* derived not
from the logic of cognition
but the oneness of meditation,
that all actions affect the
reality of Brahma

who believed in
the nonviolence of *ahimsa*
and marching minions armed in

kurta pajamas and sandals
to defeat the steel of guns,
unleashing nonviolence
upon imperial violence

who believed ignorance
to be the mere *maya*
of blind men, describing an elephant
by touching different parts,
not knowing the whole elephant
trodding over captive fences.

A small, skinny man
who was an Indian elephant
prevailing over the British lion,
ending world colonization
over four hundred ruling years

who was Gandhi
Shiva's avatar
Destroyer of empire.

8. PATHS FOUND

WALK WITH RUMI

I start out on this road,
call it love or emptiness.
I only know what's not here.
– Rumi

Walk with Rumi upon the desert sand
where caravans travel down endless roads
of silken belts through golden caliphates
when their journey treks under the stars of
of Arabian nights
            and Scheherazade seeks
love to be at the end of the journey
as told in tales of love and fortune.

For believers, the road is formless
no longer attached to the ground as
rock dissolves to sand and sand to air
and air to spirit
            and no words heard
of jet set princes and skyscraper cities
or barrels of oil to soil desert dunes.

For believers, the road has no name
made by zealous empires to extend claim
or mullahs of nations to issue fatwas
for sectarian dissenters
             for the desert
is the Jannah of wandering Bedouins
though Shams said you cannot understand.

So be a believer in the pathless path
and walk with Rumi through endless space
to traverse the world in all ten directions
no sign heeded, no compass needed
for the journey ahead
                              under the sun to shine
over green oases and brown continents
blue oceans and poles of white
                                        as you
ride the wind detached even of Rumi
(not to worry for he will understand)
and dissolve into the water of life
and fire of energy
                        for all the elements
are of you and you of them as you
abandon form and become pure spirit
in the infinite here and eternal now.

SIDE WITH JESUS

Ask some day to whom you pray –

Jesus or Christ. Whether to choose

Jesus of peace crucified by empire

or Christ of war crusaded by empire?

If you doubt what I mean

dare to ask Constantine.

SIT WITH BUDDHA

Mara
swoops down
from the sixth heaven
with demons of dread
fire and fury
with daughters of desire
samsara defiled.

Buddha
sits unmoved
at the bodhi tree
smiling in silence
fourth jhana of equanimity
peace and purity
nirvana undefiled.

Done to
shelter all buddhas
facing dread and desire
to stay the middle way
between life or death
accepting neither side
of one world to abide.

WALK WITH LAO TZU

Walk in the Tao with Lao
not here, not there
but everywhere.

You know without knowing,
Tao is always unknown
by knowledge not lasting.

You name without naming,
Tao is always unnamed
by language not lasting.

When severed from Tao,
you walk with straw dogs
among ten thousand things.

When united with Tao,
you walk along the path
of earth into heaven.

Tao is like wood
when uncarved left for good
but when carved used for bad.

Tao is the cosmic egg
from which all things emerge
to which all things return.

Tao is the pure calm
before the storm of action
when nature is inhumane.

Tao is what it is
not for you to have
because it has you.

So walk with old Lao Tzu
while knowing and trusting
Tao as life's primal goo.

WALK WITH BLACK ELK

You have two roads in two directions
decisions to make forward or back
for the human soul of blood red
or forbear the dead in night black.

Walk with Black Elk on the Red Road
the Chanku Luta with native fathers
Americans before America
unnamed people of an open land

traveled by pilgrims of all calling
with peace pipe in hand to smoke
the holy grass of prairie land

seated in the sweat lodge of fire and water
in the Inipi of purification
blessed by the father Wakan Tanka

hunted south-north to buffalo grounds
worshiped north-south to ancestor world
at the end of living and dying.

Walk not the Black Road
the Chanku Sapa against your native brothers
east-west to the prison of reservations
west-east from the prism of laws and bureaus

the trail of fallen tears and overseers
bringing disease and war along the way

across the new American empire of
terrorism since fourteen ninety-two

the end of tribal nations on rations and
degrading recompense from casino trade
of wampum beads intricately woven
for dollars of paper in gaming and used

to buy and burn indigenous souls
and cloud a virgin land with black smoke
shrouding a people once proud and free
their civilization in misery.

WALK THE WAY WITH CARE

I am somewhere lost in the wind.
– Rumi

Walk the way with proven prophets:

    Jesus to Jerusalem and heaven
    Muhammad to Mecca and paradise
    Buddha to the Bodhi Tree and nirvana
    Lao Tzu into the Tao
    Moses to the Chosen Land
    Black Elk on the Red Road.

Or walk on the sweet side with:

    Marius the Epicurean to
    smell the dew of new life in spring
    hear the leaves from high in trees
        see the opening of sunlight ahead
        feel the way upon fertile ground
        taste the sweet nectar of flowers.

Or walk on the wild side with:

    Rumi the Sufi mystic to
    venture up into the vista and
    ride the whirlwind of Allah
    do the dervish dance with Shams
    wander out in formless sand
    release spirit in open sky.

But always walk the way with care:

   Don't hold onto your birth place where
   they know not who you are or what you mean
   although wanting to be of good health to them
   while reciting the Whitman song of self

     back in Kansas where the wind is
     but weather and possible rain
     for flat fields of harvesting grain.

   Don't ride the wayward road of careless Beats
   sullied children of New York city streets
   seeking refuge from oppressive culture
   by extolling chaos of Bill Burroughs

     this aged heroin addict who
     to Mexico City fled
     then shot his wife in the head.

Don't listen with Vivekananda to
Madam Calve sitting on her veranda
and lamenting her fear of becoming a
drop of water lost in the Indian Ocean

     she with Rudyard Kipling
     sipping cold Lipton Tea
     British always first to be.

Don't stride down from the mountain with
Zarathustra to foretell the world
of the epochal noontide call
to the Valkyrie beat of *ubermensch*

Nietzsche spurned and turned away
condemned to end his last twelve years
in the night of madness and fears.

Don't stay with Robinson Jeffers
warning those who would partake in
Mother Church and Father State and
seek reclusive truth knowing it's

     lonely to be an adult as a
     poet to California children
     who lay on pictured sunny shores
     Rainbow Sandals on their heads
     bodies tanned with Natural Glow
     arms tattooed with Taijitu
     chanting Tao as young monks do.

Don't plead poetic with Leonard Cohen
singing on high from his tower of song
commiserating with Hank Williams
how all love was lost and what went wrong

     still singing high from his tower
     clinging to poetic power
     as his song goes through the night
     lamenting every love not right.

Don't click on beguiling media
providing pleasure by algorithms
according to your demographics
with no further choices needed

where instant truths are anecdotes
what becomes viral is virtue
and how you ever want to look
as your pixel best on Facebook.

So know the sacred path up the mountain
is narrow with weeds and rocks under foot
yet followed by gods and heroes of old
of journeys taken in long told stories

all with the vision of purpose
to find the promised direction
on long roads going everywhere
to perfection or perdition

trusting in Egyptian wind gods
of all four directions, with Amun
the creator who rules as the great
Protector of the Road for purity

of men blown by relentless wind
their bodies scattered in the sand
and of lifting their souls up to
heavens hosted by all known gods.

STAR WALK

Do not feel lonely. The entire universe is inside you.
– Rumi

Looking far, he was on a star
Looking down, he was on the ground
I saw that pale adventurer of a thousand faces
The intrepid traveler from ten thousand places.

I asked,
from where he comes
to where he goes.
He replied,
from star stuff he comes
to dark matter he goes.

I asked,
if he were a god or avatar.
He replied,
a soul with common sense
of cosmic providence.

I asked,
about Eden
and of Heaven.
He replied,
'twas a mishap
not on the map.

I asked,
about the purpose of life
and finality of death.
He replied,
both are mystery
solved only by me.

I asked,
if I could learn
about his sojourn.
He replied,
no need for me to ask
'tis already my task.

Yes, I am the unnamed traveler of all places
Joseph Campbell's hero of a thousand faces
Reliving a life of changing form
Whereby go the old as youth reborn.

9. FAITH FOUND

VITRUVIAN MAN

Vitruvian Man stands exultant
in lines and curves before our eyes,
drawn at the dawn of the Renaissance
by the bright genius of Da Vinci

to project the perennial ideal of:
perfect bodies of perennial heroes,
Hercules unchained for pagan tasks
and naked beauty of Aphrodite

to reject the dogma of original sin:
shame of nudity told in Genesis
peccatum originale declared by St. Augustine
bodies whipped in the fires of Dante's Inferno

to elect not man contrived as:
an avatar exalted in cult
superhero created by culture
athlete, celebrity or film star
übermensch Atlas of Ayn Rand

but as the perfect and universal man
in a simple drawing of a single figure
framed by square and circle in harmony

fulfilling axiomatic requirements
in the geometry of the universe
and cosmology of all known heavens.

So always will stand Vitruvian Man
first envisioned in the Axial Age
to be rediscovered by every sage

and reborn as the Phoenix from the
the ashes of human predilection
but to rise again as perfection.

INSTANT BEING

Lightning flashes, sparks shower.
In one blink of your eyes, you have missed seeing.
– Mumonkan, 21

You live in the instant always here now
beginning when born and ending dead
flowing and recurring in your being

and your instant is ordinary
like a drop of water appearing
and disappearing before your eyes.

And, your instant can be extraordinary
waking you and touching your soul
    flashing, searing
    Paul's epiphany on the road to Damascus
Moses's hearing God through the burning bush
Mohammad's hearing Allah in a mountain cave.

You can see out to the universe
into the glow of sprinkled star dust
    bristling, blinking
as cosmic background radiation
sparkling like Indra's string of jewels.

You can breathe in the cosmic wind
streaming across the universe
    unstoppable, endless

like Einstein's energy of mass
breaking the contours of your mind.

You can extend and stay in the instant
free from past regret or future hope
        empty, unattached
unburdened by the luggage of karma
enlightened by the Buddha's dharma.

You can see through the universe
of fourteen billion time-space years
                immediate, boundless
timeless as Tillich's eternal now
endless as Mendelbrot's fractal.

You can do all things possible
in the world of instant being.

NIGHT TRAIN

I ride the train into night
   one-way ticket in hand
   destination unknown

departure from

familiar shapes and sounds
of livelong holding and

faces seen and voices heard
in a world once to abide

all now falling back
   as the rays of yellow light
   recede over my shoulder

then gone
   past a last station
   and glimmer of light

to my destination
one-way, no track back

straight like Eddington's arrow
passing through linear time

no curve or circle of return
not like light, unbending to mass.

I sit alone
   motionless in empty space
   of Einstein's no-gravity box

as the train accelerates
leaving stars and worlds behind

and I realize no returning
no turning back to what is gone.

Questions flash by like
streaking meteorites:

Where to go in a future unknown?
Is this the end or new beginning?

More questions flash by as a
cyclone of panic swirling

– No, stop everything!

and I jump up to find
the emergency chord

– None found!

and crash into the wall
   falling to the floor
   helpless and still

then look up to see

my father and mother
   from a past long ago
   here in this world

opaque but illuminated
in their presence

then a voice from afar:
I saw eternity the other night;
calm as it was bright.

My mind becomes a void
fathomless and formless

no questions to ask
no answers to give

while staring out the window
into dark of emptiness

free of past regrets and future hopes
free of desire and wondering

   my mind at rest
   destiny set

      no going back
      no getting off

         no matter
         all is well.

FEARLESSNESS

In the fabled face of death
Ever blowing heroic breath
Champions of fear management
Strut across the stage
Speak of Invictus
masters of fate and captains of soul
no wincing or crying, heads unbowed.

As if heroes can run and win the race
    an Olympia at which to vie.

As if deniers had a stalwart place
    a Valhalla at which to die.

As if death was a foe to be smitten
Or an epic story to be written
    a soul superordinated to arise and meet God
    a baby reincarnated to return and cry aloud
                    a soldier to fight and die for country
                    a leader to bequeath a legacy.

Yet, fearless abiders take not flight nor fight
regarding death to be not denied or cried.

They stay the country courtyard with Thomas Gray
when there was little doubt what it was about.

Like Robert Frost they knew it was not old or new
so did their best with miles to go before they rest.

ONENESS

Never mind our mind
great but bound to break:

bound to laws that break
thought into categories of
identity, contradiction and excluded middle

bound to laws that break
matter into forces of
diffusion, entropy and dark energy.

Wonder about our world
not of law but with awe:

there is here, then is now
parts whole, degrees circle
end begin, begin end
black and white gray
earth with heaven.

Fathom our faith
not dual but mono:

there always is a world of one,
which we are in and of
as stuff of stars and planets,
all the same substance of
cosmic consciousness and
matter/energy existence

there never is a you and me,
only a we to be looked over
by our monkey cousin in the tree
who laughs at all our laws of
distinctive thought and matter.

and there never is an i and it,
only a universal all around
Brahma who sits on a lotus flower
to delete human lines creating
edges of space and lapses of time
and to repeat natural circles
ensuring eternal return

all while with knowing smile
as we float below through
an ether of oneness.

OPENINGS

There is a crack in everything, that's
how the spirit gets out from the
shell of self and swell of ego

   escaping
   from the edges of the vise
   closing in upon the mind
   and into open spaces
   of transcendent consciousness.

Black holes leak bits of energy
a photon at a time running
into space to save itself

   everlasting
   information not lost as
   photons unite with protons
   combined afar to light darkness
   and fused to give birth to a star.

Martin Luther King shines new light
on caste of mind made black by white
to see blind justice had by all

   freedom
   God's children free at last, free at last
   marching together on the rainbow
   of colors seen in a natural world.

The Seed ascends from earth
through the black grime of decay
and up to the blue of the sky

  renewal
   of the Phoenix arising from
   the ashes of the burning earth
   to regenerate life thought lost.

The Avatar descends from above
to save humanity from greed for
empire and dominion of nature

   redemption
   for one chance left to a species
   to save itself from itself
   and the world of its making.

Such is the opening of openings
to attendant freedom and renewal

as energy of spirit
breaks through the cracks of matter

and radiates in all ten directions
where possibilities are infinite.

BREATHING

Long-distance runner breathes deep
defies the torpor of mass
fuels exhausted lungs and legs
crossing still the finish line

as a butterfly takes pollen
gives life to future flowers
flutters in the morning sun
displaying all the colors

as Pavarotti exhales
attains exact vibrations
transforms raw sound to music
producing beauty of song

as a guru meditates world
opens consciousness of mind
closes suffering of self
having bliss of nirvana

as the cosmic wind blows dust
brings into space energy
moves galaxies and pebbles
creating the universe

so as she now breathes in here
sleeps through the uncertain night
joins me still when at the dawn
making sure my day of love.

OF MYSELF

I loafe and invite my soul.
– Walt Whitman, Song of Myself

I am more than energy
scattered across formless fields
of remnant radiation or
vaporous string theory,
rather like Indra's jewel
connected eternally

more than probability
of statistical error
and past indeterminacy
of Heisenberg's formula,
rather like Einstein's set dice
always rolling up seven.

I am the mass of matter,
the Mandelbrot fractal of
eternal divine design

the body of vital life,
the Darwin culmination
of supreme evolution

the perfect universal form,
Vitruvian man standing
in circle and square as one

the seed bee among flowers,
pollinating stigmata
to beget buds of heaven.

I am the last perfection
of everything everywhere,

avatar of Homo Deus.

ACKNOWLEDGMENTS

My faith stays strong with Carol, my guardian lifelong, who stands with me.

Poems appearing elsewhere are:

"Anthropic Plea," *Illinois State Poetry Society*, September 2023.
https://illinoispoets.org/poems0923.htm#NotAlone.

"Breathing," *Distilled Lives,* Anthology by Illinois State Poetry Society, 2024, V. 7, p. 66.

"Fearlessness," *International Journal of Fear Studies*, 2019, Vol 1, p. 44,
University of Calgary Library PRISM (digital open-access),
Microsoft Word - IJFS vol 1 no 1 2019.docx (ucalgary.ca).
chrome-extension://efaidnbmnnnibpcajpcglclefindmkaj/https://
prism.ucalgary.ca/server/api/
core/bitstreams/8a1dfd11-4d9d-4b0a-8802-a393adea5ebe/content.

"The Honking of the Geese," *Quilted*, Poetry Nation Anthology, Eber & Wein: New Freedom PA: 2024.

"Openings," Illinois State Poetry Society, May 2024.
https://illinoispoets.org/poems0524.htm#Openings.

"Places," *Distilled Lives,* Anthology by Illinois State Poetry Society, 2024, V. 7, pp. 64-65.